This Planner
belongs to:

_____

_____

WEEKLY PLANNER

Monday

Tuesday

Wednesday

Thursday

Friday

Weekend

TO-DO LIST

DON'T FORGET

NOTES

WEEKLY PLANNER

Monday

Tuesday

Wednesday

Thursday

Friday

Weekend

TO-DO LIST

♥
♥
♥
♥
♥

DON'T FORGET

NOTES

WEEKLY PLANNER

Monday

Tuesday

Wednesday

Thursday

Friday

Weekend

TO-DO LIST

DON'T FORGET

NOTES

WEEKLY PLANNER

Monday

Tuesday

Wednesday

Thursday

Friday

Weekend

TO-DO LIST

DON'T FORGET

NOTES

WEEKLY PLANNER

Monday

Tuesday

Wednesday

Thursday

Friday

Weekend

TO-DO LIST

DON'T FORGET

NOTES

WEEKLY PLANNER

Monday

Tuesday

Wednesday

Thursday

Friday

Weekend

TO-DO LIST

DON'T FORGET

NOTES

WEEKLY PLANNER

❧ Monday ❧

❧ Tuesday ❧

❧ Wednesday ❧

❧ Thursday ❧

❧ Friday ❧

❧ Weekend ❧

TO-DO LIST

- ♥
- ♥
- ♥
- ♥
- ♥

DON´T FORGET

NOTES

WEEKLY PLANNER

Monday

Tuesday

Wednesday

Thursday

Friday

Weekend

TO-DO LIST

DON'T FORGET

NOTES

WEEKLY PLANNER

Monday

Tuesday

Wednesday

Thursday

Friday

Weekend

TO-DO LIST

DON'T FORGET

NOTES

WEEKLY PLANNER

❧ Monday ❧

❧ Tuesday ❧

❧ Wednesday ❧

❧ Thursday ❧

❧ Friday ❧

❧ Weekend ❧

TO-DO LIST

♥
♥
♥
♥
♥

DON'T FORGET

NOTES

WEEKLY PLANNER

Monday

Tuesday

Wednesday

Thursday

Friday

Weekend

TO-DO LIST

DON'T FORGET

NOTES

WEEKLY PLANNER

Monday

Tuesday

Wednesday

Thursday

Friday

Weekend

TO-DO LIST

DON'T FORGET

NOTES

WEEKLY PLANNER

Monday

Tuesday

Wednesday

Thursday

Friday

Weekend

TO-DO LIST

DON'T FORGET

NOTES

WEEKLY PLANNER

Monday

Tuesday

Wednesday

Thursday

Friday

Weekend

TO-DO LIST

DON'T FORGET

NOTES

WEEKLY PLANNER

Monday

Tuesday

Wednesday

Thursday

Friday

Weekend

TO-DO LIST

DON'T FORGET

NOTES

WEEKLY PLANNER

Monday

Tuesday

Wednesday

Thursday

Friday

Weekend

TO-DO LIST

♥
♥
♥
♥
♥

DON'T FORGET

NOTES

WEEKLY PLANNER

Monday

Tuesday

Wednesday

Thursday

Friday

Weekend

TO-DO LIST

DON'T FORGET

NOTES

WEEKLY PLANNER

❧ Monday ❧

❧ Tuesday ❧

❧ Wednesday ❧

❧ Thursday ❧

❧ Friday ❧

❧ Weekend ❧

TO-DO LIST

♥
♥
♥
♥
♥

DON´T FORGET

NOTES

WEEKLY PLANNER

Monday

Tuesday

Wednesday

Thursday

Friday

Weekend

TO-DO LIST

DON'T FORGET

NOTES

WEEKLY PLANNER

Monday

Tuesday

Wednesday

Thursday

Friday

Weekend

TO-DO LIST

DON´T FORGET

NOTES

WEEKLY PLANNER

Monday

Tuesday

Wednesday

Thursday

Friday

Weekend

TO-DO LIST

DON'T FORGET

NOTES

WEEKLY PLANNER

Monday

Tuesday

Wednesday

Thursday

Friday

Weekend

TO-DO LIST

DON'T FORGET

NOTES

WEEKLY PLANNER

Monday

Tuesday

Wednesday

Thursday

Friday

Weekend

TO-DO LIST

DON'T FORGET

NOTES

WEEKLY PLANNER

Monday

Tuesday

Wednesday

Thursday

Friday

Weekend

TO-DO LIST

DON'T FORGET

NOTES

WEEKLY PLANNER

Monday

Tuesday

Wednesday

Thursday

Friday

Weekend

TO-DO LIST

DON'T FORGET

NOTES

WEEKLY PLANNER

Monday

Tuesday

Wednesday

Thursday

Friday

Weekend

TO-DO LIST

DON´T FORGET

NOTES

WEEKLY PLANNER

Monday

Tuesday

Wednesday

Thursday

Friday

Weekend

TO-DO LIST

DON´T FORGET

NOTES

WEEKLY PLANNER

❧ Monday ☙

❧ Tuesday ☙

❧ Wednesday ☙

❧ Thursday ☙

❧ Friday ☙

❧ Weekend ☙

TO-DO LIST

♥
♥
♥
♥
♥

DON'T FORGET

NOTES

WEEKLY PLANNER

Monday

Tuesday

Wednesday

Thursday

Friday

Weekend

TO-DO LIST

DON'T FORGET

NOTES

WEEKLY PLANNER

Monday

Tuesday

Wednesday

Thursday

Friday

Weekend

TO-DO LIST

DON'T FORGET

NOTES

WEEKLY PLANNER

❧ Monday ❧

❧ Tuesday ❧

❧ Wednesday ❧

❧ Thursday ❧

❧ Friday ❧

❧ Weekend ❧

TO-DO LIST

- ♥
- ♥
- ♥
- ♥
- ♥

DON'T FORGET

NOTES

WEEKLY PLANNER

Monday

Tuesday

Wednesday

Thursday

Friday

Weekend

TO-DO LIST

DON'T FORGET

NOTES

WEEKLY PLANNER

Monday

Tuesday

Wednesday

Thursday

Friday

Weekend

TO-DO LIST

DON'T FORGET

NOTES

WEEKLY PLANNER

Monday

Tuesday

Wednesday

Thursday

Friday

Weekend

TO-DO LIST

♥
♥
♥
♥
♥

DON'T FORGET

NOTES

WEEKLY PLANNER

Monday

Tuesday

Wednesday

Thursday

Friday

Weekend

TO-DO LIST

DON'T FORGET

NOTES

WEEKLY PLANNER

Monday

Tuesday

Wednesday

Thursday

Friday

Weekend

TO-DO LIST

DON'T FORGET

NOTES

WEEKLY PLANNER

Monday

Tuesday

Wednesday

Thursday

Friday

Weekend

TO-DO LIST

DON'T FORGET

NOTES

WEEKLY PLANNER

Monday

Tuesday

Wednesday

Thursday

Friday

Weekend

TO-DO LIST

DON´T FORGET

NOTES

WEEKLY PLANNER

Monday

Tuesday

Wednesday

Thursday

Friday

Weekend

TO-DO LIST

DON'T FORGET

NOTES

WEEKLY PLANNER

↣ Monday ↢

↣ Tuesday ↢

↣ Wednesday ↢

↣ Thursday ↢

↣ Friday ↢

↣ Weekend ↢

TO-DO LIST

♥

♥

♥

♥

♥

DON'T FORGET

NOTES

WEEKLY PLANNER

Monday

Tuesday

Wednesday

Thursday

Friday

Weekend

TO-DO LIST

DON'T FORGET

NOTES

WEEKLY PLANNER

Monday

Tuesday

Wednesday

Thursday

Friday

Weekend

TO-DO LIST

DON'T FORGET

NOTES

WEEKLY PLANNER

Monday

Tuesday

Wednesday

Thursday

Friday

Weekend

TO-DO LIST

DON'T FORGET

NOTES

WEEKLY PLANNER

Monday

Tuesday

Wednesday

Thursday

Friday

Weekend

TO-DO LIST

DON´T FORGET

NOTES

WEEKLY PLANNER

Monday

Tuesday

Wednesday

Thursday

Friday

Weekend

TO-DO LIST

DON´T FORGET

NOTES

WEEKLY PLANNER

Monday

Tuesday

Wednesday

Thursday

Friday

Weekend

TO-DO LIST

DON'T FORGET

NOTES

WEEKLY PLANNER

ᔐ Monday ᔐ

ᔐ Tuesday ᔐ

ᔐ Wednesday ᔐ

ᔐ Thursday ᔐ

ᔐ Friday ᔐ

ᔐ Weekend ᔐ

TO-DO LIST

DON'T FORGET

NOTES

WEEKLY PLANNER

❧ Monday ❧

❧ Tuesday ❧

❧ Wednesday ❧

❧ Thursday ❧

❧ Friday ❧

❧ Weekend ❧

TO-DO LIST

DON´T FORGET

NOTES

WEEKLY PLANNER

Monday

Tuesday

Wednesday

Thursday

Friday

Weekend

TO-DO LIST

DON'T FORGET

NOTES

Weekly Planner

Monday

Tuesday

Wednesday

Thursday

Friday

Weekend

TO-DO LIST

DON'T FORGET

NOTES

WEEKLY PLANNER

Monday

Tuesday

Wednesday

Thursday

Friday

Weekend

TO-DO LIST

DON'T FORGET

NOTES

WEEKLY PLANNER

Monday

Tuesday

Wednesday

Thursday

Friday

Weekend

TO-DO LIST

♥
♥
♥
♥
♥

DON'T FORGET

NOTES

My Notes and Sh*t

Notes

Notes

Notes

Notes

Notes

Notes

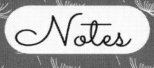

Notes

Notes

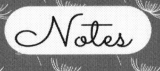

Notes

Notes

Notes

Notes

Notes

Notes

Notes

Notes

Notes

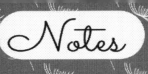

Notes

Notes

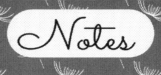

Notes

Notes

Notes

Notes

Notes

Notes

Notes

Notes

Notes

Notes

Notes

Notes

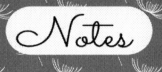

Notes

Notes

Notes

Notes

Notes

Made in the USA
Las Vegas, NV
06 December 2024

13506013R00068